Dedicated to the next generations:
May you have faith in yourselves and faith in our ability
to make a better world, working together.
DW

To Darcy, Kimberlee Campbell, and Mike Ottertail,
who told me the story. And to Anne, who sent me to them.
HMO

Text copyright © 2025 by Darcy Whitecrow and Heather M. O'Connor
Illustrations copyright © 2025 by Natasha Donovan

First edition 2025

Library of Congress Catalog Card Number pending
ISBN 978-1-5362-2945-5

25 26 27 28 29 30 CCP 10 9 8 7 6 5 4 3 2 1

Printed in Shenzhen, Guangdong, China

This book was typeset in Scala Pro.
The illustrations were created digitally.

Candlewick Press
99 Dover Street
Somerville, Massachusetts 02144

www.candlewick.com

EU Authorized Representative: HackettFlynn Ltd.,
36 Cloch Choirneal, Balrothery, Co. Dublin, K32 C942, Ireland.
EU@walkerpublishinggroup.com

ACROSS THE ICE

How We Saved the Ojibwe Horse

Darcy Whitecrow and Heather M. O'Connor
illustrated by Natasha Donovan

CANDLEWICK PRESS

IT IS A COLD, SNOWY NIGHT at Lac La Croix First Nation. Nookomis and Mama sent us to bed hours ago. But how can we sleep on such a special night?

We're not the only ones awake. The house is filled with the buzz of aunties and uncles and cousins.

Nookomis spies us tiptoeing out. "They're not here yet, little ones."

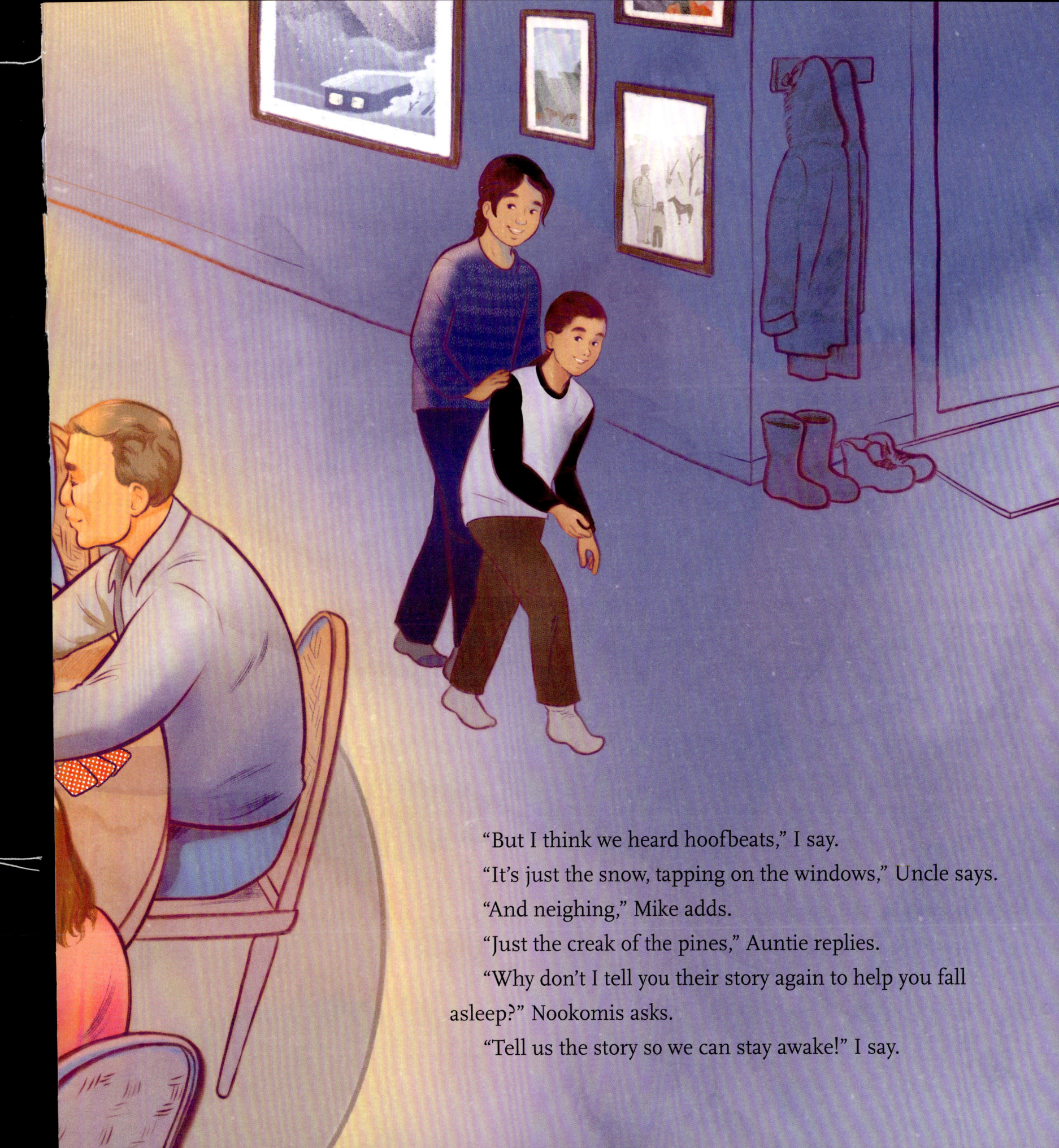

"But I think we heard hoofbeats," I say.

"It's just the snow, tapping on the windows," Uncle says.

"And neighing," Mike adds.

"Just the creak of the pines," Auntie replies.

"Why don't I tell you their story again to help you fall asleep?" Nookomis asks.

"Tell us the story so we can stay awake!" I say.

"Many years ago," Nookomis begins, "long before cars and trucks and snow machines, our people shared this land with herds of wild ponies. The ponies were curious and friendly. They were easy to catch and quick to learn.

"In the winter, they helped us run our traplines, pull sleighs, and haul wood. In the spring, they carried us to our summer camps. Then we turned them loose to wander free and have their foals in the summer. When fall came, we would find them again.

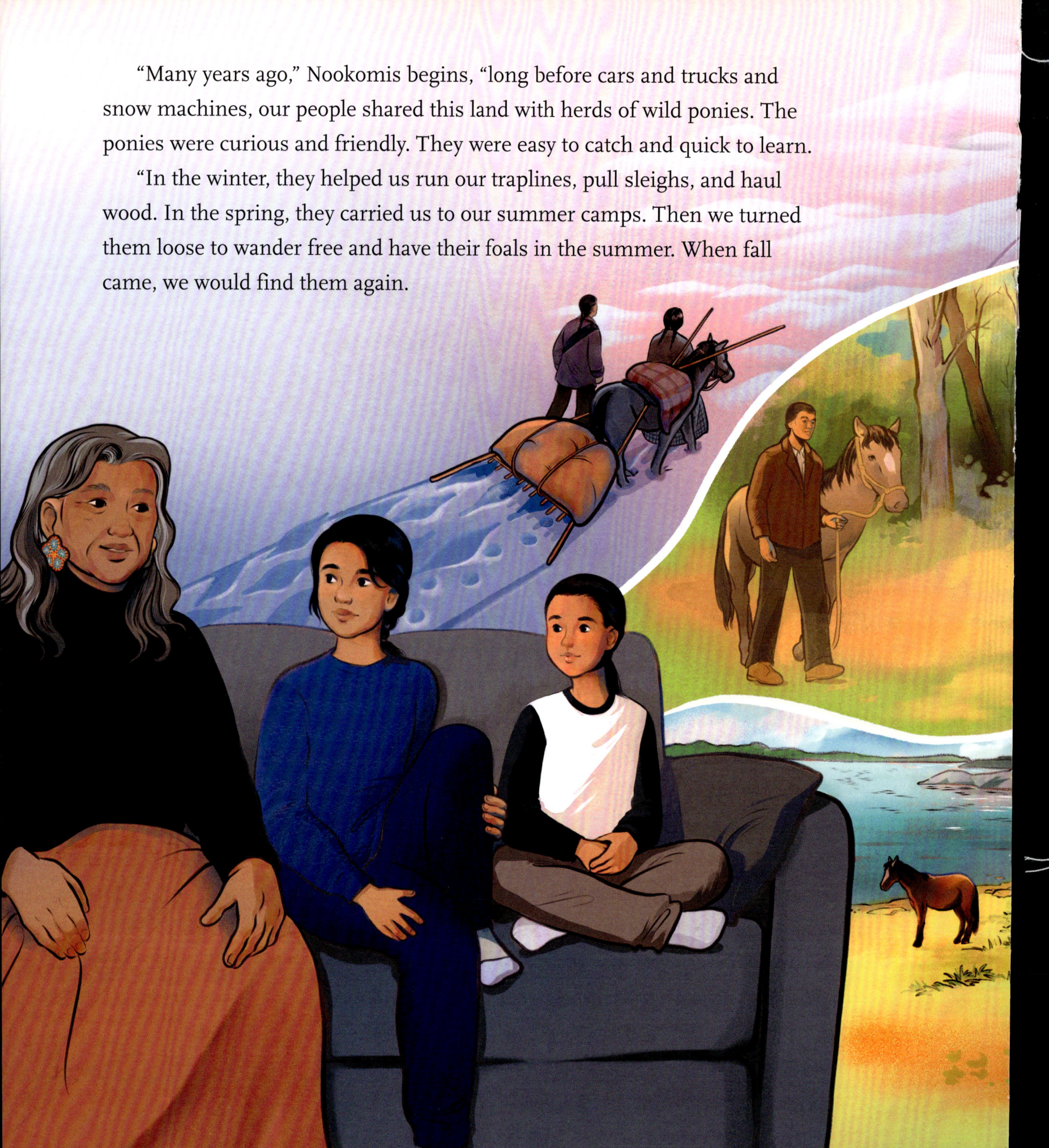

"But by the time I was born, most of the ponies were gone. Only four remained, roaming the woods here at Lac La Croix. Their names were Bizhiki and Lillian, Dark Face and Diamond.

"The government didn't like our little wild ponies. They called them a nuisance and a health hazard. They were going to shoot them.

"We couldn't let that happen. Our ancestors had bred these ponies for many generations. They were our spirit animals. Our friends. They were the last of their kind. We had to save them. But how?

"A man called Fred Isham, one of our relations from the reserve at Nett Lake, offered to help. He said he'd take the horses across the border to a farm in Minnesota, where they could live in safety and freedom. But getting them there was harder than we'd thought."

"Why was that, Nookomis?" Mike asks.

"Well, in those days, there was no road to Lac La Croix. The only way to move the horses over the border into the United States was across the lake.

"One cold day, when Lac La Croix was good and frozen, Fred and some friends hauled an empty horse trailer over lakes and along snow-mobile trails and around islands and across the Canada–United States border until they reached us. Then all we had to do was catch the horses and put them in the trailer."

"But that was harder than you thought. Right?" I say.

"It sure was!" Nookomis says with a laugh.

"It took a few hours to find the horses. And just when you thought you had them cornered, they'd quick-trot past.

"We were able to catch the two older ponies without too much trouble, even though they hadn't been handled much lately.

"The two young ones? Well, they'd never been handled at all. At first, they reared and shied and bucked. Took a bit, but we finally got halters on them.

"Then we loaded them up and waved goodbye. It's been forty years now, but I can still see that trailer, disappearing over the ice. Last I ever saw of them," she says sadly.

The room grows quiet for a moment, then Nookomis picks up the story again.

"The farmer had promised to give our ponies room to run and good food to eat. But . . ."

"That was harder than he thought!" we all say together.

"Like the moose and the deer, the Ojibwe horses had always eaten bark and twigs and wild grass. So the rich hay the farmer gave them made them sick. Eventually, the ponies adjusted and settled into their new home. But the story doesn't end there.

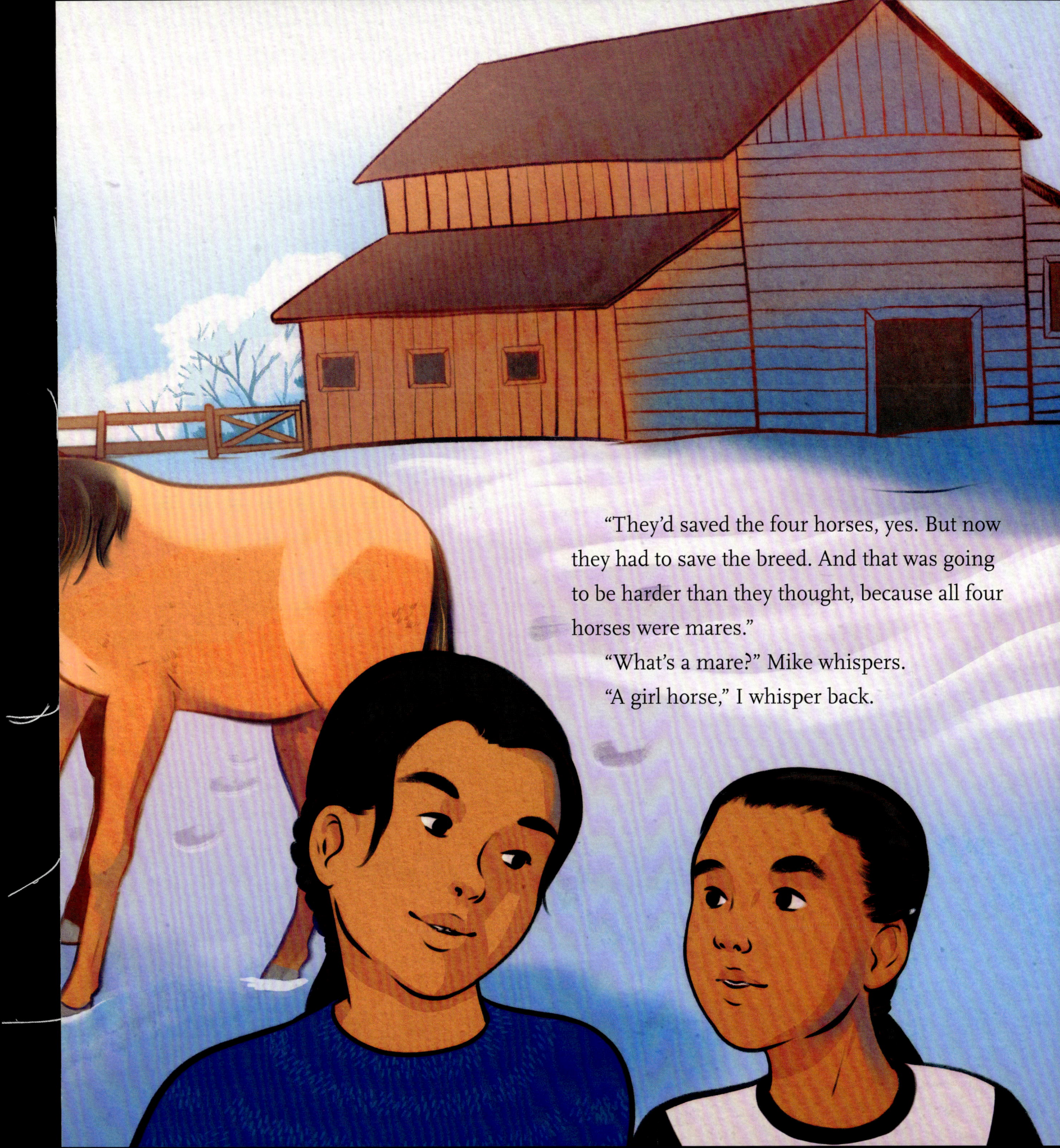

"They'd saved the four horses, yes. But now they had to save the breed. And that was going to be harder than they thought, because all four horses were mares."

"What's a mare?" Mike whispers.

"A girl horse," I whisper back.

"The farmer bred the mares with a mustang stallion."

"A stallion's a boy horse," I whisper to Mike.

"The mares all had foals," Nookomis continues.

"Babies," I add.

"And slowly, over many years, the herd began to grow. The breed became known as the Lac La Croix Indigenous pony, to honor our role in saving those last four mares. But now we call them Ojibwe horses, to honor our ancestors.

"Now we're starting our own little herd at Lac La Croix with five mares and a stallion from out west.

"It's a long, cold road from Alberta to northwestern Ontario. But their trip home will soon be over."

As Nookomis finishes her story, we all sit in silence thinking about the journey of the Ojibwe horses. That's when I see the headlights.

"Look!" Mike yells. "They're here!"

"Now you are part of the story, too. Someday, you will tell your grandchildren how you stayed up late to welcome our horses home."

"And that wasn't hard at all," I say.

AFTERWORD

Most people have never heard of the Ojibwe horse. It's a wild breed that once lived among the Ojibwe people of northwestern Ontario and northern Minnesota. Elders say that the horses have always been here.

Winters are cold and snowy north of Lake Superior. Ojibwe horses developed special adaptations to help them survive. When the weather turned cold, their coats grew thick and shaggy. These small, powerful horses had long, flowing manes and tails to swish away flies and small, hard hooves that could handle rocky ground. Like deer, they could digest bark, roots, and wild grass.

The horses helped the Ojibwe people run their traplines. In exchange, the Ojibwe people provided food and shelter for the horses in the winter.

When settlers arrived, the horses were often rounded up and destroyed. By 1977, the herds of thousands were reduced to just four mares, living at Lac La Croix First Nation, next to Quetico Provincial Park.

The daring "heist across the ice" launched a long conservation process. Today, there are about 180 Ojibwe horses, including a small herd at Lac La Croix First Nation.

To learn more about the Ojibwe horse, visit the *Canadian Encyclopedia* (https://www.thecanadianencyclopedia.ca/en/).

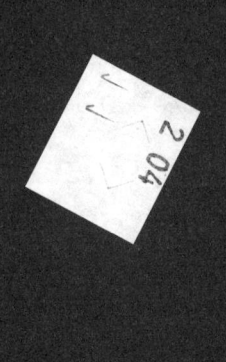